Why do [illegible]

written by Herbi[illegible]man

illustrated by Jackie Harland,
Beccy Blake and James Sneddon

Contents

Why do cats purr?	2
How do cats say hello?	4
How well do cats hear?	6
Can cats really see in the dark?	8
Why is a cat's tongue so rough?	10
Why do cats have whiskers?	12
Is smell important to a cat?	15
Why do cats sleep all day?	16
How is a cat like a camel and a giraffe?	18
Do cats really have nine lives?	19
Have cats always been kept as pets?	20
Glossary	23
Index	24

Why do cats purr?

Most people think cats purr because they're happy. They certainly do purr for this reason. Kittens do it when they're feeding. The mother cat often purrs too.

But cats will also purr when they're sick or injured. Purring doesn't seem to be just about happiness. It seems to mean that a cat is feeling something really deeply.

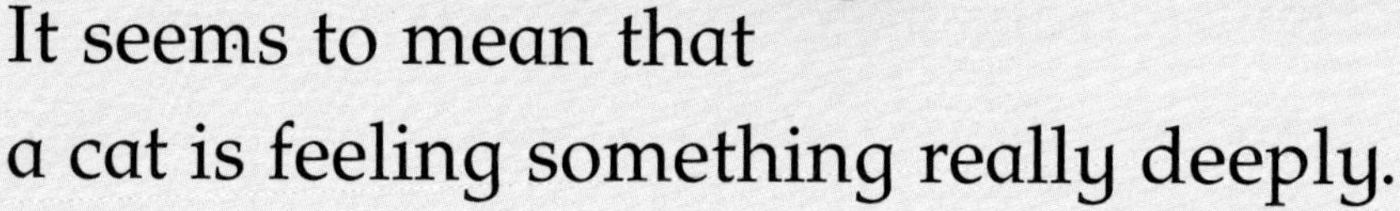

Purring isn't the only noise cats make. They use up to 16 cat sounds that seem to mean different things.

For instance, a little trill seems to mean that a cat is pleased to see you, and hissing means that it is feeling threatened.

How do cats say hello?

Cats will often greet their owners (or other, friendly cats) by rubbing the side of their head, lips, chin or tail against them.

The reason for this is that there are **scent glands** in the cat's head, lips, chin and tail. By rubbing against things, the cat leaves its own scent on them. It makes sure that the people and things that it likes have a familiar smell.

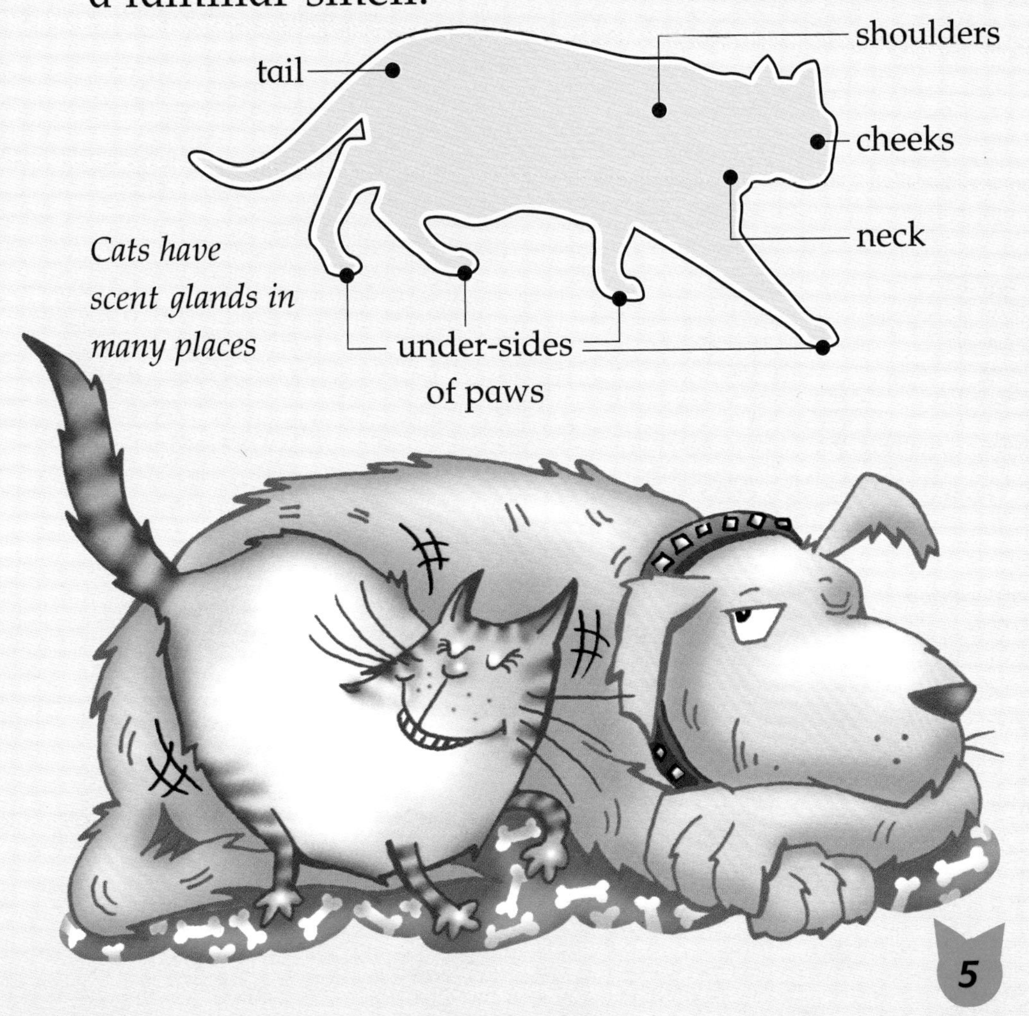

Cats have scent glands in many places

How well do cats hear?

Cats can hear quieter sounds than you can. A cat can hear a mouse walking over straw or your footsteps coming down the road.

A cat's ears work the same way as human ears, but scientists think the part of the brain that deals with sound works faster in a cat.

It's also a fact that your ears have six muscles around them, but a cat's ears have about 30 muscles around them! Because of this, cats can turn their ears towards a sound and this helps the cat to hear well.

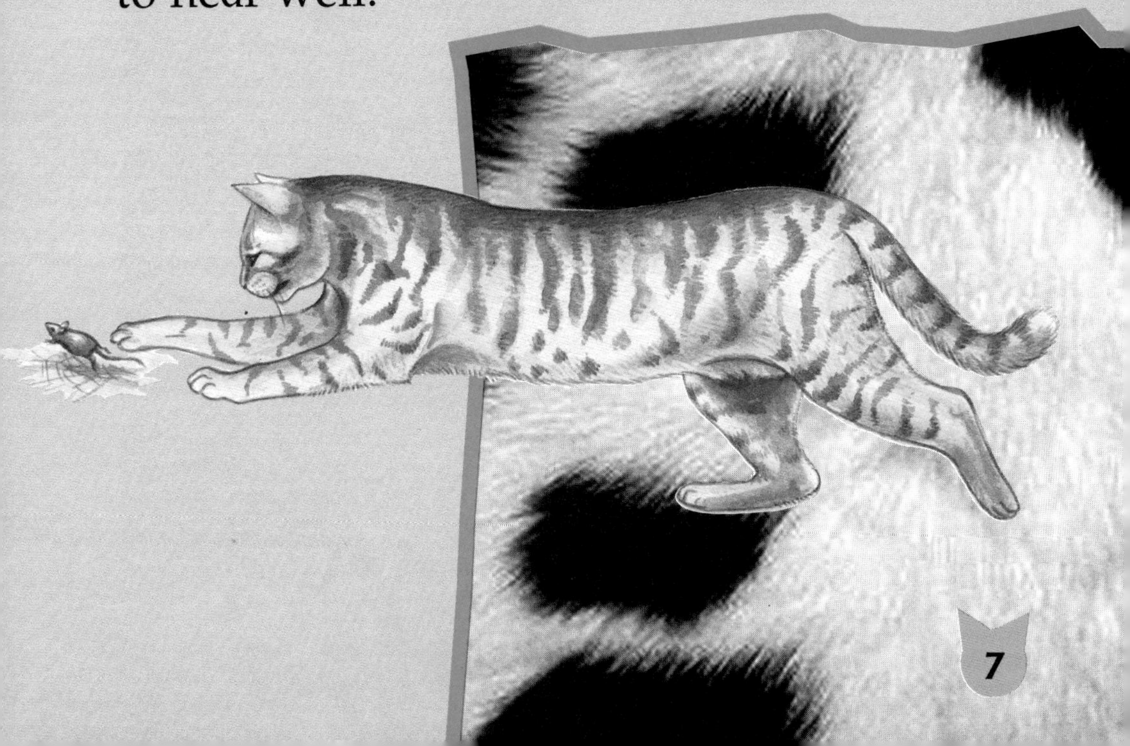

Can cats really see in the dark?

Cats can't see in total darkness. No animal can.

But since cats have to hunt at night, their eyes can take in far more light than yours can. This means that cats can see far better after dark – in fact, about six times better than you can.

A cat's eyes are extra sensitive to light because there is a layer of tiny crystals inside them. It is this layer that makes a cat's eyes glow in car headlights at night.

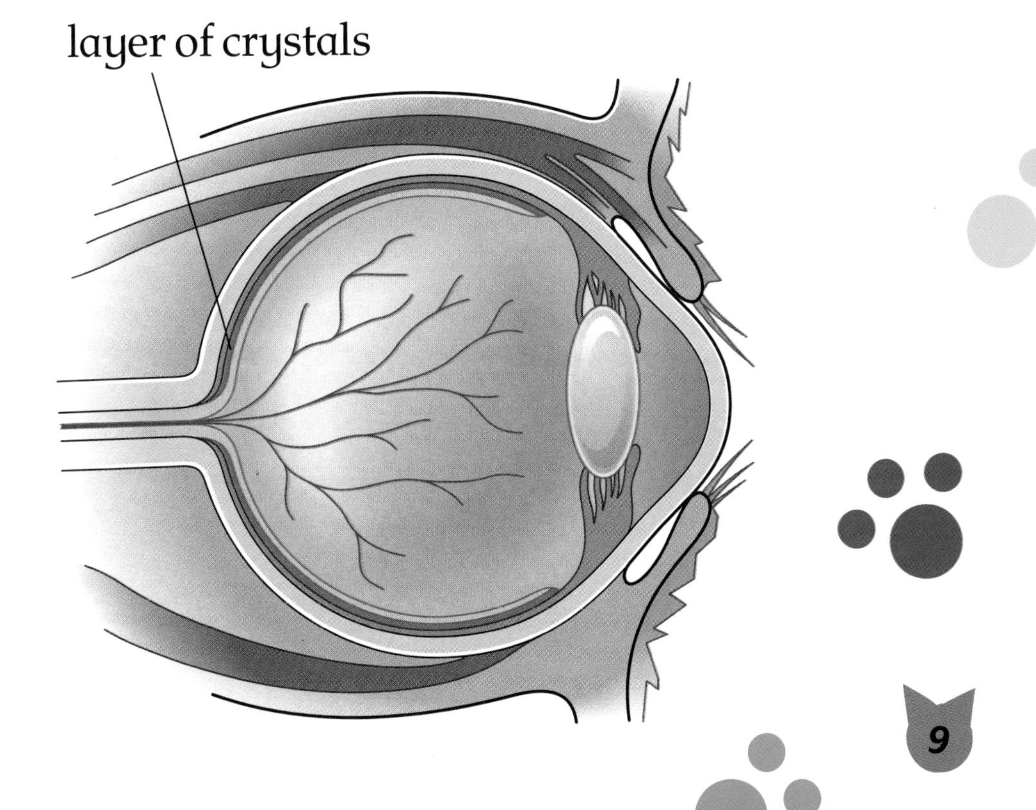

Why is a cat's tongue so rough?

There is a patch of spines on one part of a cat's tongue which helps it lap milk. The rest of the cat's tongue is rough to help it groom itself.

Cats wash themselves thoroughly, especially after eating, to get rid of their own scent. When cats hunt, it is important that their enemies or **prey** do not know they are there. A cat's scent would be a warning to the prey.

The cat's rough tongue also helps it to remove loose hairs from its coat.

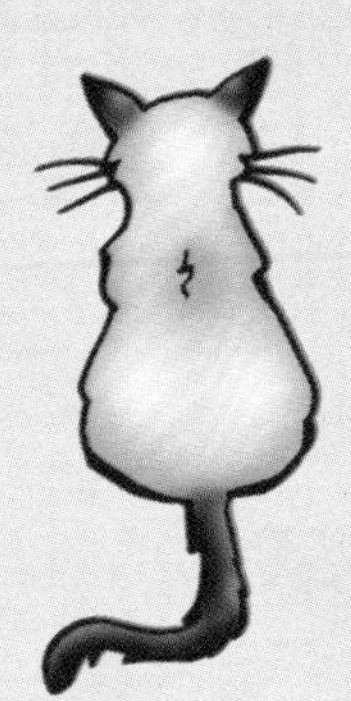

Why do cats have whiskers?

Cats' whiskers aren't for decoration. They help a cat find its way about. If a cat's whiskers will fit through a gap, so will the cat!

But a cat's whiskers are important for other reasons too. They can detect very deep pitched sounds – sounds that are too low to be heard in the usual way, even by a cat. They can also sense air moving around them. This means cats can tell when possible danger is coming. The smallest **vibration** or movement in the air alerts the cat.

Cats also use their whiskers to send signals to other cats. When the whiskers are flattened back, a cat is giving up the fight.

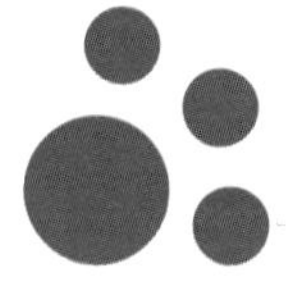

Is smell important to a cat?

Like most animals, cats have a better sense of smell than people do. Cats decide whether food is safe to eat by smelling it. If their noses are blocked so that they can't smell, cats have been known to starve to death rather than eat. So smell is very important indeed to a cat.

Why do cats sleep all day?

Cats sleep for most of the day because they hunt at night. They sleep very lightly so that they can wake up quickly and be alert.

When cats go out at night, they roam, fight, mate and most of all they hunt. Even a well-fed pet cat likes to hunt for sport. This is shown by the fact that most cats will kill shrews, even though they never eat them. They don't seem to like the taste!

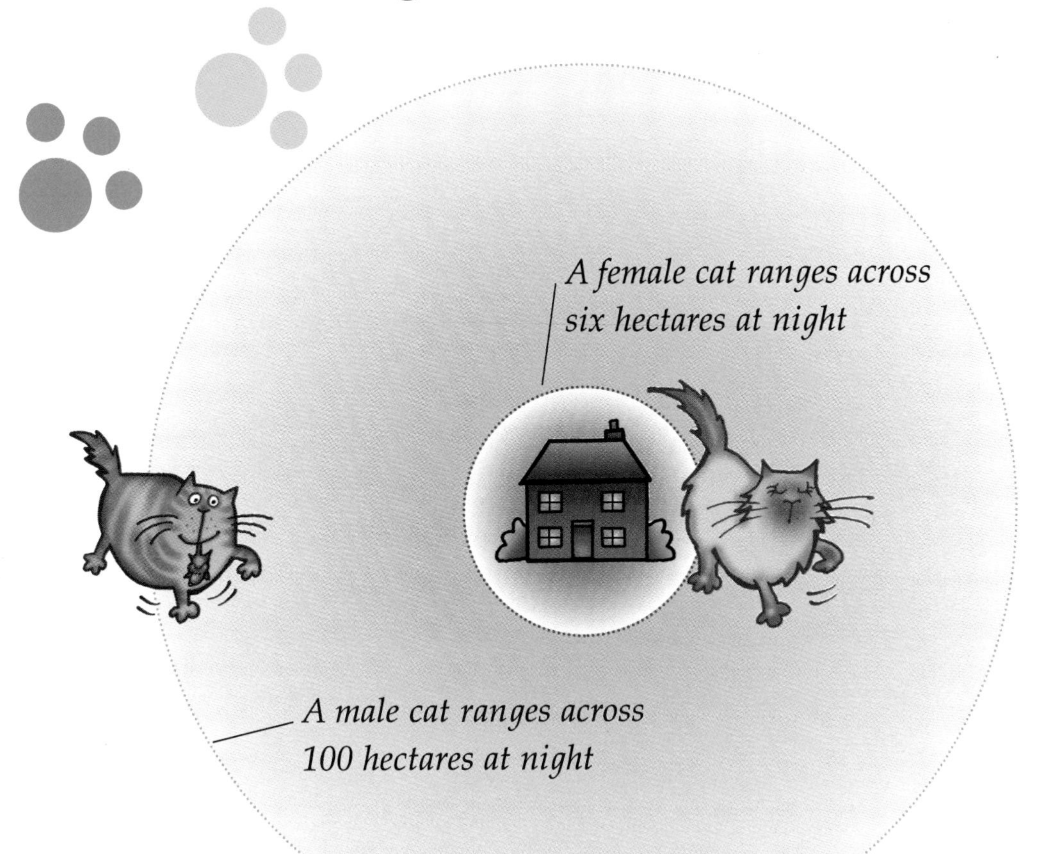

How is a cat like a camel and a giraffe?

A cat, a camel and a giraffe all run in the same way. Cats, who walk on their toes, run by moving first the front and back legs on one side, followed by the front and back legs on the other side. Camels and giraffes are the only other animals to run this way.

Do cats really have nine lives?

Cats only have one life like all other animals. But when they get sick, they often lie around, and won't move at all. This helps them save their energy, but it can make them look nearer to death than they really are.

A sick cat may seem dead, but then it may suddenly recover. This is why some people in the past used to think that cats have nine lives.

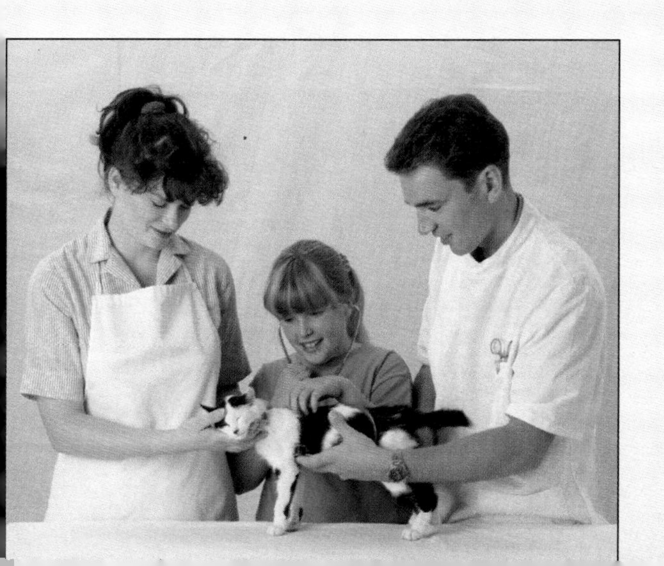

NOTE: A sick cat should always be taken to a vet. Only a careless owner would leave it to get better on its own.

Have cats always been kept as pets?

Not always. In Ancient Egypt, about 2500 BC, cats were worshipped as gods. They were kept as pets from 1500 BC.

So, cats have been kept as pets for the past 3500 years.

Bastet, the cat goddess

2500 BC

Cats worshipped in Ancient Egypt

1500 BC

Cats kept as pets in Ancient Egypt

1000 BC

Cats taken to Europe

500 BC

Pet cats become common across Europe

55 BC

Pet cats brought to Britain by the Ancient Romans

Egyptians didn't keep cats to catch rats or mice. They had special house snakes for that.

In Ancient Egypt, if a pet cat died, the owner shaved off his own eyebrows to show how sorry he was. The cat was then carefully **mummified**, like a king, and often had its own little coffin.

A mummified cat

There have been wild cats in Britain since prehistoric times, but pet cats were first kept by the Romans who invaded in 55 BC.

These are cat footprints found in the Roman town of Chelmsford in Essex. They are on clay tiles that must have been made in Roman times, left out to dry in the sun, and a cat walked across them! Nobody can be sure if this was somebody's pet, but it seems very likely.

Glossary

mummify a way to stop a dead body decaying

prey animals that are hunted for food

scent glands small organs in a body that produce the smell by which the animal is known

vibration tiny movements in the air or some other substance

Index

brain 7
Britain 21, 22

Chelmsford 22
crystals 9

danger 13

ears 7
eating 11
Egypt 20–21
eyes 8–9

food 15, 17

hearing 6–7
hiss 3
hunting 8, 11, 16–17

kittens 2

mouse 6, 21
muscles 7

night 8, 9, 17
noises 2–3

purr 2–3

rats 21
Romans 22
running 18

scent 5, 11
(see also *smell*)
scent glands 5
shrews 17
sleep 16
smell 5, 15
snakes 21

tongue 10–11
trill 3

vet 19
vibration 13

washing 10–11
whiskers 12–14
wild cats 22